Rod Decker Reports on Utah Politics & LDS Church

Introduction

Welcome to Gospel Tangents. I'm your host Rick Bennett. Please consider donating or purchasing a transcript by going to our website https://GospelTangents.com/shop . You'll help support other documentaries and podcasts such as this.

They say there are 2 topics you aren't supposed to talk about: religion and politics. We're going to talk about both! Rod Decker has covered Utah politics for nearly 4 decades. Following his retirement from KUTV News (Channel 2) in Salt Lake City, Utah, Rod has written a political history of the state. We will talk about how much the LDS Church has influenced Utah politics, and how Utah went from a swing state to one of the strongest Republican strongholds in the nation. Does the LDS Church control Utah politics? Check out our conversation....

Contents

Introduction 2

Utah: Most Religiously Polarized Electorate 4

Downwinders & Utah's Fight Against the Feds...........................15

Does the LDS Church Control Utah Politics? 24

How Utah Politics are Different than the Nation 33

Additional Resources: 39

    Elder Steven Snow, Church Historian 39

    Greg Prince on Gays & the Mormon Church......................40

    Dr. Paul Reeve on Black Mormon History in Utah 41

Epilogue 42

Utah: Most Religiously Polarized Electorate

Introduction

I'm excited to introduce Rod Decker. If you've lived in Utah, you probably know who he is since he was a staple of KUTV Channel 2 News for nearly four decades. Rod recently retired, which has given him time to put together a political history of Utah. Utah has been known as the most reliably republican state in the nation, but at one time, Utah was a swing state. Rod will tell us how that change occurred. Check out our conversation....

Interview

GT 0:52 Welcome to *Gospel Tangents*. I have an amazing guest. If you've lived in Utah, you must know my guest. So could you go ahead and introduce yourself?

Rod 1:02 I'm Rod Decker.

GT 1:03 And why would you be famous?

Rod 1:06 I used to be on TV. I'm retired now.

GT 1:09 You're very humble, I think. I do have people who are outside of Utah that may not be familiar with you, but you were at Channel 2 forever.

Rod 1:20 I was at Channel 2 for, I don't know, 37 years, I believe? Yeah. 37 years.

GT 1:28 So you were just a staple of the Utah news market.

Rod 1:31 Well, if you hang around long enough, then people get to know who you are.

GT 1:37 So tell us about your book. You've got a book here.

Rod 1:40 This is called "Utah Politics: the Elephant of the Room."[1] It came out about the first of July. I've been writing on it for 10 or 15 years, and it's about Utah politics.

GT 1:54 Go ahead. Let's learn a little bit about your background. Did you go to school here?

Rod 2:00 I grew up in Utah. I went to the University of Utah and graduated. I went to graduate school at the University of Chicago, where I was a wretched graduate student. I was a soldier in Vietnam. I attended Harvard for a year on what's called a Nieman Fellowship. It's a wonderful thing. They just give you some money and let you loaf and then I worked at the *Deseret News* for eight years as an editorial writer and columnist a long time ago. Then I worked at Channel 2 for 37 years.

GT 2:38 That's awesome. One of the things I loved about your book is you give us a history of politics here in Utah. Can you kind of give us a history from, say statehood to...

Rod 2:55 Okay, let's start before. This is about political history.

GT 3:02 Right.

Rod 3:02 Utah political history divides into three phases, three periods: territorial period, the mainstream period which started at statehood, and lasted till 1976, and the Republican ascendancy since 1976.

Rod 3:24 Here's the secret. If Latter-day Saints and Americans agree about sex and families, then Utah is like everybody else politically. If they disagree, then Utah's different from everybody else politically. In the territory, they disagreed over polygamy. Utah was a pariah, kept away from statehood. They threw people in jail. They took the vote away from Utah women. Within Utah, there was a Latter-day Saint party and a non-Mormon party. The Latter-day Saint party almost always won. The non-

____

Mormon party pretty often got their way anyway, because the federal government was on their side.

GT 4:13 Did they have names of these parties back then?

Rod 4:15 Yeah. The People's Party was the Latter-day Saint party, and the Liberal Party was the non-Mormon party.

GT 4:22 Okay.

Rod 4:24 Statehood: Utah changes its party so that they become Democrats and Republicans, and they mixed them up so that there were Latter-day Saints and non-Mormons in both parties; strong two party competition. Utah for 80 years was in the American political mainstream. There were 20 presidential elections, 1896 to 1972, Utah voted with the majority of Americans, that's for the winner 17 times. Only three states voted for more winners in those elections than Utah. Utah had two-party competition. Utah state government usually swung with national elections. It's hard to believe, but Utah was ordinary politically, kind of in the middle.

GT 5:21 It's really hard to believe that now. Because I remember in your book, you said that the Utah was really a swing state.

Rod 5:28 Well, it was in those days. Political science professor Frank Jonas taught at the University of Utah. There was a saying, "As Maine goes, so goes the nation," because Maine was on the very east coast and its returns came in first. People watched Maine and they thought usually the nation went that way. He made a joke about it. He said, "As the nation goes, so goes Utah," because Utah voted mostly with the nation. Utah was a normal state. In 1976, it changes. Utah gives up its tradition of voting mostly for winners, and votes most strongly for the loser, President Gerald Ford, Republican, of any state. In the next four elections, including that Ford, Reagan, Reagan, first Bush, Utah votes, the most strongly republican of any state. Utah had never voted most strongly for a candidate of either party before. It becomes enduringly and strongly

Republican. It has only voted Republican since then, and it has been the most Republican state in seven of 11 presidential elections since then.

Rod 6:47 Okay, we were normal, normal, normal, normal, normal, whoops, we're Republican, Republican, Republican, Republican. It spreads throughout the state government. Our congressional delegation is now five-sixths Republican. We have one Democrat. He was just elected. He's in his first year. Before that it was all Republican. The governor is Republican. The state legislature is Republican. Salt Lake City is Democratic, but the state is seriously and thoroughly Republican. It has been for years and it doesn't seem to matter what happens. We stay Republican. Donald Trump was sort of an exception. Okay, what happened?

Rod 7:39 We now have kind of what we had in the territory. We have a Latter-day Saint party. They're called Republicans instead of the People's Party. We have a non-Mormon party. They're called the Democrats instead of the Liberal Party. Latter-day Saints vote 70% Republican. I told you how on 11 elections, Utah was the most Republican state in seven of them. If only non-Mormon votes had counted, no Mormon votes get to count, Utah is the most Democratic state for Al Gore. Utah is the second most Democratic state for Barack Obama both times, even against Mitt Romney. Mitt Romney just gets wiped out in Utah. Utah is the fifth most Democratic state for Hillary Clinton. Utah would have gone for Reagan the first time. Other than that Utah been would have been Democrat.

GT 8:43 So you're saying that if we only counted non-Mormon votes.

Rod 8:46 Only non-Mormon votes. Utah is the most religiously polarized electorate of any state. We have Latter-day Saints. We have non-Mormons. We call them Democrats and Republicans, but pretty much it's a religious divide. Okay, so what happened? Well, first Latter-day Saints changed. Latter-day Saints changed in 1976. That was the election after *Roe v. Wade*. *Roe v. Wade* was the Supreme Court decision that overturned abortion laws, including Utah's abortion laws.

GT 9:22 That was in 1973, right?

Rod 9:23 Yes, 1973. The next presidential election was 1976. You're right. Before that we were ordinary. After that we were Republican. Now, it wasn't just that. *Roe v. Wade* came after a decade and a half or more of the sexual revolution. Sexual intercourse began in 1963.

GT 9:53 In 1963 it began?

Rod 9:54 {Quotes the poem *Annus Mirabilis*}

Sexual intercourse began
In nineteen sixty-three
(which was rather late for me) -
Between the end of the "Chatterley" ban
And the Beatles' first LP.

Up to then there'd only been
A sort of bargaining,
A wrangle for the ring,
A shame that started at sixteen
And spread to everything.

Then all at once the quarrel sank:
Everyone felt the same,
And every life became
A brilliant breaking of the bank,
A quite unlosable game.

So life was never better than
In nineteen sixty-three
(Though just too late for me) -
Between the end of the "Chatterley" ban
And the Beatles' first LP.

Rod 10:26 That's *Annus Mirabilis* by Philip Larkin.[2] But he's right. Sex changed in the 60's. The sexual revolutionaries cried Sex, Drugs and Rock 'N Roll. An American woman born in 1942 has a 30% chance of having sex out of marriage before she's 21. An American woman born in 1955 has a 72% chance of having sex out of marriage. In 1968, 75% of Americans who have an opinion say that sex out of marriage is either always wrong, or almost always wrong. In the early 1980's, as low as a third say that. Opinions changed. Conduct changed. People married less. In 1960, 72% of American adults were married. Now it's 48%. People had more sex outside of marriage. People had fewer babies, but more of those babies outside of marriage. In 1960, fewer than 5% of American babies were born outside of marriage, now it's 42% of all American babies are born outside of marriage.

Rod 11:51 So, you've got a big change. Frank Furstenberg, who's a family sociologist says the American, and more broadly, the Western--it happened in Europe, too and Australia and Canada and New Zealand. America and more broadly the Western family changed more in the last half of the 20th Century than in any comparable span period of time in history. It was fast family change and family change in a direction the Church of Jesus Christ of Latter-day Saints didn't like. They believe in the traditional family.   They believe in the old morality that sticks up for the traditional family. Essentially, sex should happen only between a married man and woman. No other sex. They stuck to that. They emphasized it. They preached more about it than they had before. They issued The Family, a Proclamation to the World saying how important traditional families were, and by extension, how important (they call it chastity,) not having sex before marriage, how important faithfulness in marriage is, how important it is for traditional families and the morality that supports them. They got whopped.

[2] Philip Larkin (1922-1985) See https://www.wussu.com/poems/plam.htm

Rod 13:20 The Latter-day Saints don't realize what's happened to them politically in Utah, but here's what's happened. Abortion, pornography, censoring cable television, birth control for teenagers without telling their parents, gay marriage, one after another, and in every one of them, Utahn's debated and fought and argued for two or three years. Then the legislature voted almost surely, in most of the cases, they voted the considered preference of a majority voters, the Latter-day Saint majority. And then in every case, federal judges came along and said, "No, no, you lose." In every single case, and in some of the cases, they invoked new interpretations of the Constitution. In birth control it was statute, but in most of it, it was Constitution and most of it was an evolving Constitution. So, on an issue that was of fundamental importance, they argued, they debated, they decided, it got thrown out time after time. They became Republicans and serious Republicans. Non-Mormons face this Latter-day Saint Republican juggernaut and they become Democrats.

GT 15:05 So it sounds to me like what you're saying here is up until, pretty much probably 1973, Utahns were a swing state.

Rod 15:16 Normal.

GT 15:18 They were a swing state, but it's been kind of between the tumultuous sexual revolution in the '60s, and kind of the climax was really with the *Roe v. Wade* in 1973.

Rod 15:31 Okay. The court decisions made it political. They had opposed the sexual revolution, but what the heck.

GT 15:40 Everybody was opposing it, or a lot of people were.

Rod 15:41 Yeah. Everyone felt the same, says the poem. Well, Latter-day Saints didn't feel the same. But it wasn't so much a political issue. It became a political issue with *Roe v. Wade*. Political scientists have looked at it. That's what's gave rise to the Christian Right was *Roe v. Wade*. Before that Evangelicals were not especially political. Afterwards, they became seriously political and Evangelicals, Latter-day Saints, Pentecostals became a serious part of the Republican base. Here's what happened. Conservative religions became Republican. In America, Evangelicals, Pentecostals, Latter-day Saints were about 25% of the population. In Utah, Latter-day Saints are two-thirds of the electorate. So what was a shift in America was a tsunami in Utah.

GT 16:45 Okay.

Rod 16:45 And it still determines the outcome of our politics.

GT 16:52 Well, now, I want to ask you this question. I don't know if you know, Dr. Matt Harris.[3] He's a professor from Colorado State-Pueblo. But he's done a big biography on Ezra Taft Benson.[4]

Rod 17:02 Yeah.

GT 17:03 Benson was a very ultra, right Republican.

Rod 17:08 He was a strongly conservative man.

GT 17:10 So can you talk a little bit? Because he was very forceful in the 1960s. Can you talk about his influence on Utah politics?

Rod 17:19 I think he had some influence while he was alive. Well, actually, before he became president. Near as I could tell, once he became president, he shut up about politics. Part of it was he got senile toward the end. But part of it was, he thought politics were important, but when he got to be president, he said, "Well, I'm running the Lord's work here. That's even more important." I think. I never actually heard it. I never actually talked to him. I think that because he talked about politics a lot before he was president, and hardly at all after.

GT 18:06 Exactly. Because I know Matt's documented a lot of the General Conference talks, especially because he was a staunch anti-communist.

---

[3] See our interview at https://gospeltangents.com/2019/02/how-ezra-taft-benson-joined-eisenhower-part-8-of-13/
[4] Can be purchased at https://amzn.to/2JGia7G

Rod 18:14 He was pro-McCarthy.

GT 18:16 Right.

Rod 18:16 At Channel 2 where I worked--I didn't do it, but we did an interview with him, where he said, "Joseph McCarthy was doing the Lord's work." I mean, he was for Joseph McCarthy who is a very controversial figure. Most people say he was a witch hunter is the normal thing. Okay. There is a theory, I'll think of her name in a minute. She's from Missouri and she writes about writes about Mormons. Jan something.

GT 18:55 Jan Shipps?

Rod 18:56 That's it. She wrote an article saying what changed Mormons was Ezra Taft Benson. I just don't agree with that. I think Ezra Taft Benson had some influence while he was talking and politicking. But I don't think his influence has lasted. His conservatism was different from current Latter-day Saint conservatism. His conservatism was anti-federal government, which they are now, but it was strongly anti-communist. His son was state coordinator for the John Birch Society.

GT 19:33 Yeah, Reed Benson.

Rod 19:34 Yeah. Ezra Taft Benson appeared on the cover of the John Birch Society magazine. His conservatism was for small government, though, he went in as Secretary of Agriculture, and then he came out. While he was in there, agriculture subsidies grew. He talked about cutting them, but, in fact, they grew. But he was, in theory, a "cut the government" man. He was strongly anti-communist. Now, current Latter-day Saint conservatism has hardly anything to do with anti-communism. I mean, Latter-day Saints aren't communists, but there is not a Proclamation to the World: Anti-Communism. There is a Proclamation to the World: The Family.[5]

---

[5] See https://www.churchofjesuschrist.org/study/manual/the-family-a-proclamation-to-the-world/the-family-a-proclamation-to-the-world?lang=eng

Rod 20:27 There were two sociologists who looked at General Conference talks from 1970 to 2009. Is that right? 1979 to 2009.[6] Family was the second most important topic. Only Jesus Christ was more important. I don't think anti-communism even made it. I doubt it.

GT 20:55 But it sure was big in the 60s.

Rod 20:56 Yeah, it was big in the 60s, but the 60s were the 60s and they went away. The family's still here. The sexual revolution is still here. It's ongoing. We're still arguing over gay marriage. Parents still worry about what their teenage sons and daughters may be doing or the influences that may come on them. People still worry about pornography. That's here. That's now. That's something that affects people's lives, and, I think, affects Latter-day Saint folks.

GT 21:33 Well, I just want to follow up with one more question on President Benson because he was such an anti-communist. What do you think he would think about our current President's approach towards Putin and Russia?

Rod 21:46 Well, Putin isn't a communist, so I don't know what he would think. I would think he would have difficulty with President Trump's morality, and Latter-day Saints have difficulty. Latter-day Saints voted 76% in 10 elections from 1976 through 2012, Utah Latter-day Saints voted 76% Republican. Seven out of 10 times, they were the most Republican state. For Donald Trump, they voted 46% Republican. Now they didn't vote for Hillary Clinton, they voted for Evan McMullin.

GT 22:27 So if you combine Trump and McMullin, is that close to 76%?

Rod 22:31 Yeah, that's about what it is. Evan McMullin got 32% of the Latter-day Saint vote.

GT 22:37 He even beat Hillary Clinton?

---

[6] Gordon Shepherd and Gary Shepherd. A Kingdom Transformed: Early Mormonism and the Modern LDS Church. Second edition. Salt Lake City: University of Utah Press. 2016. https://amzn.to/2onxRJ5

Rod 22:39 Yeah, I think maybe so. Five percent of the non-Mormon vote, a few votes in Idaho, 7% in Idaho, something like that. No votes anywhere else. He was a newcomer. So, Trump bothered Latter-day Saints. The *Deseret News* said he should give up his candidacy. They editorialized against him. So, Latter-day Saints have a problem with Trump's morality, though they're getting over it evidently.

GT 23:14 Just like all the other evangelicals.

Rod 23:19 But we'll see.

GT 23:21 So really, it looks like the sexual revolution culminating with *Roe v. Wade* is really what changed Utah politics to be much more Republican.

Rod 23:33 Yes, *Roe v. Wade*, pornography, cable television, the Equal Rights Amendment--that's one that the Latter-day Saints won. The birth control for teenagers, gay marriage, just one after another, whomp, whomp, whomp. And each one of them refreshed Latter-day Saint distrust and estrangement from Washington and each one of them pushed them again into a conservative position.

Downwinders & Utah's Fight Against the Feds

Introduction

In the 1930s and 40s, the United States was involved in the race to build an atomic bomb. Many of those above ground tests took place in the Nevada desert, and fallout from the blasts fell upon southern Utah residents. As a result, Utahns have had a history of opposing the federal government. Rod Decker will tell us more about these tests, as well as Utah's love/hate relationship with the defense industry. Check out our conversation.....

Interview

GT 24:06 Well, that's very interesting. So, one of the other interesting things that I found about your book was--1973 seems like a very, what would we call that? It was kind of a cusp or a turning point there, maybe an inflection point. But even after 1973, Utah continued to elect Democratic governors.

Rod 24:29 Yes, they did. They were sort of in the habit. Cal Rampton got elected in 1964, and that was the year that Barry Goldwater was the Republican nominee and Lyndon Baines Johnson carried more than 60% of the vote, and he carried Utah and Cal Rampton became governor. Cal Rampton served 12 years and then Scott Matheson was running, and we were sort of used to Democratic governors. It took a while to trickle down. It started with the President, but we had Scott Matheson for governor. We've had five or six congressmen. We even had Frank Moss. No, he'd already gone. We didn't have senators back then. In 1976, Orrin Hatch won for the first time. But it took a while for Republicanism to get all the way through, but eventually it did.

GT 25:55 Okay, because Governor Matheson, do you remember when he left office?

Rod 25:58 He left in for 1984, I mean January of '85 is when he actually left, but '84 was the election where Bangerter was elected.

GT 26:09 I remember Governor [Matheson], and I always remember thinking, "Wow, he's a good man, even though he's a Democrat."

Rod 26:16 Governor Matheson.

GT 26:17 Governor Matheson, that's what I meant. Yeah. So '73 was kind of a turning point for national politics, but even locally, we were still...

Rod 26:26 Latter-day Saints became Republicans. It took them a while to get thoroughly Republican from top to bottom. I mean, they had Democratic governors and legislators. A lot of them were Democrats. It took a while, but eventually, they became thoroughly Republican, and Utah became pretty thoroughly Republican. Salt Lake City holds out.

GT 26:31 Well, and one of the things I remember also about your book was you said that even with the Democratic governors, a lot of times they were very strongly anti-federal government, even including Governor Matheson.

Rod 27:11 This is a different topic. It's Utah politics, but this isn't about morals, sex and families. This is different, and it isn't so much religion either. Utah used to be a defense state. Utah was hit by the Great Depression, harder than most other states. What pulled them out was World War II. After World War II, Utah had a big defense sector. For a number of years in the early 1960s, Utah had the largest defense sector of any state in proportion to its economy. I mean, we were nothing compared to California, but California was a bigger deal. Our defense sector provided a bigger percentage of jobs. We had Hill Air Force Base. We had other military installations, and we had a big rocket, a big aerial defense industry. We had Litton. We had Markon. We had Hercules. We had a lot of them.

GT 28:14 Morton Thiokol.

Rod 28:16 Yes, a lot of them, and they paid a lot of money, these manufacturing jobs. They carried the economy for a number of years in the 1960s. We were pro-defense. When they said, "We want to put nerve gas at Tooele," we said, "Yes, sir." When they said, "We want to put germ warfare at Dugway," we said, "That's a good place for it." We did that from World War II until Scott Matheson.

GT 28:52 The main reason is because we were recovering from the Depression and we needed the jobs. Is that right?

Rod 28:58 That was the start in World War II, but then even after our economy recovered, we had good years. I mean, we're talking about the Depression was the '30s, and we're in the '60s. World War II was very good years for Utah economically, and we had some good years afterwards. Our economy grew. Things were pretty good. But part of the reason, maybe the chief reason they were pretty good was the defense sector of the federal government. Mining was a big thing then, too, and people's ideas changed. In World War II, if you had a good job, that was good. But defense was a good thing to do. We believed in America. We wanted to win the war. By Vietnam, we didn't believe so much in America. We didn't particularly care whether our guys won the war, maybe. We weren't so patriotic. We weren't so pro-defense. It wasn't just us; it was the whole country. So, then there were a series of controversies that are still going on, though less than they used to, over destroying nerve gas at Tooele, over a lab to test biological weapons at Dugway. The big one, the start of them, was the downwinder issue where were the United States tested atomic bombs in Nevada. The fallout drifted over southern Utah. It was said thousands died. If you look at the scientific papers, what they can show is maybe 50 or 60 [died,] not good, but...

GT 30:52 But not thousands, either.

Rod 30:53 Not thousands either. Maybe only 10 or 11.

GT 30:57 Oh really?

Rod 30:58 I mean, you can't tell who died. A guy gets cancer and he dies, you don't know [why.]

GT 31:06 Was it because of smoking?

Rod 31:09 So yeah, what you do is they do two things. They do dosimetry. They calculate how much radiation he might have been exposed to. Epidemiology it's called. They calculate how much cancer there was against how much cancer they think there ought to have been. We end up with maybe 10, maybe 50. Now the level of proof has to be high. It has to be 90 or 95% statistically that it wasn't just bad luck. That's the way epidemiology works. Those aren't special rules to beat up on southern Utahns. That's the way it works, and by that 10 to maybe 50 or 60 died, mostly little children, a lot of childhood leukemia.

GT 31:10 Do you know Dr. Joseph Lyon by chance?

GT 31:27 He was one of my professors. I actually have a degree in statistics. He talks a lot about this in our classes.

Rod 31:27 Yes.

Rod 32:24 He was the guy. He was probably the Utah scientist who did the most.

GT 32:30 He said that most of these cancers were actually thyroid cancers.

Rod 32:34 There were two, what they call sentinel cancers: thyroid cancers, and childhood leukemia. I read his paper and I read there were some thyroid cancers, and some thyroiditis that is non-fatal that they think was caused by fallout. There were some childhood leukemias. Now they studied. They looked at everything else and they can't prove in any way that they weren't caused by radiation. But they can't show that they were. So, fallout came and caused some cancers. Maybe it caused other cancers that you can't measure because they're too few. But that's the showings of science.

Rod 33:34 There's all sorts of folklore. Fallout fell like snow and kids scraped their initials on the hoods of trucks, and the paint all got burned off, except where they scraped their initials. There's no contemporary record of any of that stuff. People got radiation sickness. I think there's no contemporary records.

GT 33:57 So it seems like a lot of these stories are little bit overblown.

Rod 34:01 Yes. There was cancer. Yes, it was a very bad thing. No, it wasn't as bad as the big stories tell. But it was a big deal in Utah. People were really upset, and a lot of people still believe that there were hundreds or maybe thousands who died. If you talked to people from southern Utah, they'll tell you they saw pink clouds. I don't think they saw pink clouds.

GT 34:33 Maybe they saw pink clouds at sunset.

Rod 34:35 Right after they saw Santa Claus., maybe. I don't know. But there aren't contemporary records of pink clouds or green clouds.

Rod 34:49 Remember when the seagulls came and ate the crickets?

GT 34:52 Yeah.

Rod 34:52 They don't talk about that so much because somebody went back and looked at all the journals. Nobody at the time said the seagulls ate the crickets. That started 10 years later. People said that the seagulls saved us. This is like the seagulls and the crickets, I think. So that was the big one and that didn't make Utah different. Everywhere people complained about defense projects. Everywhere people got angry about nerve gas and biological warfare and so forth. But Utah had, as with abortion and pornography and so forth where you had one after another, but Utah had one defense fight.

GT 35:42 So these defense fights also started in the '60s? Is that true?

Rod 35:46 Well the downwinder started in the' 60s. Now let me think. Yes, and then there was the sheep kill. It was in 1968. Rampton was governor. Some nerve gas got away from Dugway and killed about 5000 sheep and the government admitted they did it. They paid damages. Governor Rampton never talked about that.

GT 36:20 These were airplane flights over from sheep ranches?

Rod 36:24 No, it was over Dugway proving ground. They used to test nerve gas in the open and in fact they had bleachers. You would sit in the bleachers with a gas mask and watch the plane do nerve gas. You were hopefully far enough away, but you had a gas mask in case. I never did it, but that's what I read. On this test, the plane does a practice run where it puts out a fake nerve gas. It isn't really a gas, it's an aerosol. It's droplets. It puts out a fake. It does a second run putting out a fake. It does a third run putting out the real stuff and it was a fighter plane attached with the spray rig on it with a nozzle and it flies 150 feet off the ground. It flies fast so that the stuff doesn't get in where the pilot is and then it climbs and goes away. But the nozzle failed to close, so it kept dribbling nerve agent as it climbed. A storm came along and blew it halfway to the Wasatch Front. It landed on the sheep and killed the sheep.

Rod 37:38 Governor Rampton said, "Don't panic, we're okay." Then he quit talking about it after the Army said, "Yeah, we're sorry we did it, we'll pay damages. But Matheson changed the Office of Governor over it. He fought over bringing nerve gas weapons to Tooele. He fought over the repercussions of the sheep kill. He fought over nuclear waste. He fought over the downwinders and he did a lot of it, one after another. He won a lot of popularity with it. He was a Democrat. He didn't come into office looking to fight the federal government, but he found his stride fighting the federal government. He did that and he became enormously popular. Utah's had popular governors, but Matheson was popular and part of the reason he was popular--MX was his biggest fight they were going to put MX out...

GT 38:51 MX missile.

Rod 38:52 Yes, they were going to put MX out in the West desert and he fought that and helped to stop it. Ronald Reagan actually stopped.

GT 39:00 President Kimball had a big role with that as well.

Rod 39:02 The LDS Church, the Church of Jesus Christ of Latter-day Saints came out formally against putting MX out there. I'm sure that had some effect, but the main thing was Ronald Reagan didn't like the idea of putting it out there and he didn't like it. It was complicated. It had to do with arms control and so forth. He didn't like putting it out there when he was a candidate. He moved it after he was president. It was a Jimmy Carter plan, but Matheson fought that. He fought a lot of federal things. Bangerter fought some federal things. Leavitt fought, especially high-level nuclear waste on the Goshute reservation, but it was one after another. It increased. It exacerbated Utah's anti-federal government feeling.

GT 40:05 That seems to have been a very, at least in my lifetime, Utah politicians are really against federal intervention in a lot of things which relates even to things like Obamacare and things like that as well. So, this tradition has been, I guess, bipartisan, until the '60s and '70s and '80s. And then it became strongly republican.

Rod 40:30 It was not so bipartisan. Rampton was pro-federal government. He was the last governor to speak well of the federal government. He was a political child of the New Deal. He got his start in politics as a staffer for congressman Will Robinson, who was a New Deal Democrat. He believed in the federal government and Matheson, while he fought them on defense, fought them on water, over the Central Utah Project, he was with them on a lot of things. He liked things like public housing. He believed in federal grants. He had no problem with Medicaid. He worked hard on welfare, which was a huge federal issue at the time. It has sort of gone away. But he worked hard in tandem with the federal government on that. He had state programs. Democrats were skeptical on defense. Remember Democrats were the anti-Vietnam War party. They were sort of anti-military, but they were pro-federal social policy, and Matheson was that way to some extent.

GT 42:06 Interesting. So can you tell us a little bit more about this Central Utah Project? It seems like that's been a big mess.

Rod 42:21 It's a federal water project. The idea is to dam streams over in the Uintah basin, and to take water that would flow down the Colorado to the Pacific, to bring it through a tunnel through the Wasatch Mountains, to bring it over here on the Wasatch Front, and eventually it'll flow into the Great Salt Lake. It'll irrigate farms or do whatever it does in the meantime. The ideas for it went back into 1920s. Western states fought over the Colorado River water. The Central Utah Project was sort of Utah's share. The guy maybe who got it the most might have been Frank Moss, the senator. He wrote a book called The Water Crisis.[7] He talked about a project to take water from the Yukon in Canada and Alaska, run it down the canal, run a canal from the Great Lakes to the Pacific Ocean. They'd meet up and cross. There'd be an 80-foot pipe bringing water into Utah. There'd be a canal that ran across Utah. They'd pump the water up to the top of the Rockies, it'd the flow down to Texas and the Rio Grande, then it'd flow down the Colorado. He was going to re-plumb the whole continent.

GT: 44:00 Wow, that's quite a project.

Rod 44:02 That was his plan. That never happened. He did help get the Central Utah Project. It was supposed to be done in 1972. It still isn't done. It was supposed to cost 100 million bucks. It's now at about 3 billion.

GT 44:22 Holy cow.

Rod 44:26 It was done to irrigate farms. That was what the Bureau of Reclamation did. Well, we don't have any more farms on the Wasatch Front, hardly. What we've got is ranch houses, not ranches. Legally, it's complicated, so that if you use the water for drinking, the subsidy isn't so great. So it keeps going on and on, and the cost keeps going up and up. It's not clear that we need the water now that it's nearly done.

---

[7] Can be purchased at https://amzn.to/34pRQ9Y

GT 44:52 That's quite a project.

Does the LDS Church Control Utah Politics?

Introduction

There have been many charges that the LDS Church controls Utah politics. Rod Decker says the Church is involved in state politics but doesn't wield as much influence as it could. I was really surprised at his answer. Check out our conversation….

Interview

GT 45:08 Let's move on a little bit here. One of the things that I think most of my listeners will be very interested in--I know that here in Utah, especially, there's a reputation that the church is too involved in politics, especially state politics. How would you respond to that claim?

Rod 45:30 The church is somewhat involved in state politics, but it depends on what you mean by involved. Utah politics are essentially what Latter-day Saints want. Mostly that's what it is. They elect the Republicans and they control the governor and they control the legislature, and they decide what happens in Utah politics, but the church as an institution doesn't do a lot. It does some, but not a lot in Utah politics. There are two polls...

GT 46:12 Would you say the church is less involved than the critics claim?

Rod 46:16 Yeah. Now if you talk to conservative Latter-day Saint Republicans, real conservatives, they say, "They teach them correct principles and let them decide on their own." That's sort of what happens. The Latter-day Saints are conservative. They don't like Washington. They're conservative economically, and giving rise to everything else, they're conservative on moral issues. They are conservative about sex and families and morals, and that's the way they vote. That's what determines

Utah politics and that's what has determined it since 1976. So, Utah politics are Latter-day Saint politics. The church hires a permanent staff of lobbyists. They go up to the legislature and tell lawmakers what they want. The lawmakers refer to them privately as the home teachers. The home teachers came by and talked to me.

Rod 47:33 But the church doesn't get what it wants all the time. They wanted a rule to make it illegal to secretly tape an interview with your Bishop. The people said, what's this? Or secretly tape a phone call with your bishop. No, they didn't get that. They've had other things they don't they don't get, but mostly on moral issues they get what they want. Sometimes they speak. They say they only talk on moral issues. They get to say what a moral issue is. They try to speak mostly on moral issues. They don't want to appear bossy and powerful and running things. Utah legislators don't want the Church telling them what to do. Utah voters, the Latter-day Saints vote Republican. Non-Mormons vote Democratic. There are more Latter-day Saint voters than non-Mormon voters, so they win. But by and large, bishops, etc. don't tell them what to do. There are two polls. Both of them polled people of various religions. Latter-day Saints was the one that said they are least likely to hear politics from their pulpit of any religion. They say no.

GT 49:13 So compared to evangelicals, the LDS Church does stay out of politics more than say evangelicals.

Rod 49:18 That's what they say.

GT 49:20 That what LDS members say.

Rod 49:21 Yeah, they said it to pollsters. I suspect that Latter-day Saints know they aren't supposed to hear politics, and therefore they don't. But I suspect that maybe it depends what you call politics and so forth. But they say that the evidence, so far as we have evidence on the topic, is that less politics from Latter-day Saint pulpits than from any other pulpit. You say evangelicals, the most politics are on the left, the liberal churches are most likely to talk politics.

GT 49:55 Oh, really?

Rod 49:56 The conservative churches less, and the Latter-day Saints, according to these polls, least of all. They get in on things and it's hard for them. Medical marijuana.

GT 50:16 I'm glad you mentioned that. I was going to ask you about that.

Rod 50:18 They didn't want medical marijuana.

GT 50:20 The LDS Church didn't want it.

Rod 50:21 No and it's okay if it's just medical. They got involved in California and gay marriage, Proposition 8. They won this great victory, and then they just got beat up on mercilessly by lots of people. They don't want to do that anymore. They want to stay out of that sort of thing. So they didn't want to go out with a big campaign the way they might have in the old days where they'd have made statements about medical marijuana and had something read from the pulpit and had a person in each stake or ward who was supposed to move the troops. They didn't do that. Instead they said, "Well, we can work with the legislature." They can, but that made people mad, too.

GT 51:18 Yeah, I'm sure there are some people who don't quite understand what all happened with the medical marijuana issue. Can you give us some background on that?

Rod 51:25 Okay, what happened is this. It was before the legislature. I blame the legislature for this whole thing. It was before the legislature and the legislature just said, "No, we're not interested in medical marijuana." They passed a bill where kids who have epilepsy can get some hemp oil, some marijuana related oil.

GT 51:54 CBD.

Rod 51:54 Yeah, which evidently helps them.

GT 51:56 Cannabinoid, or cannabis oil.

Rod 51:57 Yeah, and they passed it. There is almost no scientific evidence on the issue, because it's against federal law [to study medical marijuana.] It's a schedule one drug. People are doing a little research now, but you couldn't do research. The feds would come and throw you in jail or give you a hard time. So, we don't know. People say it works. Maybe it does. But we don't know. But the forces for medical marijuana, they got people to say, "Yes, I use it, and it works for me, and I'm just scared to death that I'm going to hear a knock and they're going to throw me in jail because of my arthritis," or whatever it is. But the legislature wouldn't have anything to do with it. So, they gathered signatures, forced a vote of the people and the people voted for it. The LDS Church did not mount a big campaign against it.

GT 53:08 Well, let's back up a little bit because it seems like once again, the legislature was not doing the will of the people. So the people gathered signatures and said we're going to put this on a ballot.

Rod 53:18 Yeah.

GT 53:18 So once it was on the ballot, then the LDS Church tried to say we don't like this law.

Rod 53:22 Yeah, we don't like that, so they changed it.

GT 53:26 So the Utahns voted it in and then the Church made a deal, supposedly.

Rod 53:32 The Church clearly talked to the legislators and clearly worked with the legislators on the changes. It looks a little like Utah's liquor system. They may change it again so that it doesn't because marijuana is different from liquor. But what they thought they would do is have state distribution. The state would sell it.

GT 54:00 At the state liquor stores.

Rod 54:01 Like the state liquor stores.

GT 54:03 Oh, so they're not actually at the state liquor stores? Because I thought they were.

Rod 54:05 No. You've got the State Liquor Store, then you have the State Marijuana Store. You've got a state distribution point, and you go and you buy medical marijuana there if you have a prescription. It made some people really angry, but it doesn't to me. You could still get medical marijuana. You can't now because it isn't implemented yet. But the idea is you could still get medical marijuana. If medical marijuana cures your pain, then I would guess that it might cure your pain if you bought it from the state as well as if you bought it from a private outfit. But it's still against federal law. While it's one thing for the state to say, we'll turn our back if a private enterprise sells marijuana. It's another thing for the state itself to be violating federal law and selling marijuana.

GT 55:12 Is the Trump administration is going to come after Utah, do you think?

Rod 55:17 I don't know, but he may not be president by the time this thing gets into effect. So anyhow, it's still being hashed about. It isn't a moral issue the way abortion or birth control for teens without telling their parents or it isn't a family issue. I think that if they could be sure that it only went for legitimate medical purposes, I think the brethren wouldn't object too much. They're afraid that it'll leak and end up going to junior high kids or something. If they could be sure it was only legitimately used, I think their objections would not be so large. But it's got people upset.

GT 56:22 Yeah, well, definitely, because I know a lot of people have complained that, here we are. We voted this law in and then the legislature just went around and changed it. They at least allowed marijuana to be legal, but they made a lot of changes that a lot of people didn't like.

Rod 56:38 Well, okay, I don't know quite what the objections are. If you can get medical marijuana, then what's the big deal?

GT 56:48 Well, I think the original initiative said you could grow your own plants, and I think they took it out and said you've got to get it at the State Liquor Store.

Rod 56:53 No, I don't think that was it. That was in at one point, I don't know that that passed. I have stopped reporting on politics, and I don't know about current events very much. I had thought that the Grow Your Own was out, but maybe not. Maybe there was a Grow Your Own in there.

GT 57:10 I thought it was in there, but I'm not sure.

Rod 57:12 Well, you know then. Okay, there was a Grow Your Own. I admit that's a change and that is significant. The one that was big, worse, in my opinion was extension of Medicaid. They voted essentially to accept Obamacare and the legislature just said no.

GT 57:39 In the recent election.

Rod 57:40 Yeah, they voted to extend Medicaid at the same time they voted in medical marijuana. The legislature just said, "No, we won't extend Medicaid. We won't extend it. We won't adopt the Obamacare plan, even though the people voted for it. Now in the medical marijuana, you still got your medical marijuana. But in the extension of Medicaid, there are a lot of poor Utahns who don't get it. It's just gone for them. Now, the legislature had their own plan. They sent it back to the Trump administration, the Trump administration said, "No, we won't give you the waivers." So maybe they'll enact what the people want next year, after all.

GT 58:28 Yeah, because can you explain why the legislature completely subverted the ballot initiative on that, because I don't understand what their reasoning was.

Rod 58:40 Well, they believe that it will grow and over time, I can't remember the exact numbers, but Medicaid is the fastest growing part of the Utah State budget. Now, 70% is paid by the federal government, but it's gone from--up to about 20%, or maybe more. It grows and grows and grows and grows, and they say this will make it grow more and grow faster. It will make it hard to balance the budget in the future.

GT 59:17 This is a budget issue for them.

Rod 59:19 This is a budget issue.

GT 59:21 They're afraid that once the federal subsidies get over, Utah's going to be over extended because Utah's really big on balancing budgets.

Rod 59:28 That's right. This is a budget issue for them. Besides, they just don't like it. But the big thing they talk about is the budget issue. They say, "We'll expand it just for the really poor people, but we won't go to the middle-class people." The Trump administration won't do that.

GT 59:47 I guess the question then comes, isn't this a family issue? Shouldn't the church become involved as a lobbyist on this?

Rod 59:53 Well, the church doesn't consider this a family issue. The church gets to say what a family issue is and what they'll get involved in.

GT 1:00:00 And they want no part of this.

Rod 1:00:01 They just don't say anything about it. The Catholic Church says this is a family issue and they have a lobbyist up there who was lobbying for extension of Medicaid. Some of the other churches lobbied for that. The Church of Jesus Christ, they worked on medical marijuana to change that, but they had nothing to say about extension of Medicaid.

GT 1:00:35 Well, and they haven't said anything about the gerrymandering. That was another thing that passed.

Rod 1:00:39 Well, it hasn't happened yet. We don't know what they're going to do with that. They haven't done anything to that yet, and they may not.

GT 1:00:46 Because I know that's a big issue, especially with non-Mormons, because basically they've carved up Salt Lake County into four districts to dilute the Democratic vote.

Rod 1:00:57 Yes. The fundamental issue is this. Utah has four congressional districts, and about a third of Utah's vote is Democratic, maybe a little more. So is it fair? You could say every district ought to be about the same as Utah. Then every district is Republican. Or you could say, the Democrats ought to get one. Democrats want one, they want a Democratic district. The Republicans don't want to give them one. Now, it would make a difference of a couple of legislative seats. But unless you happen to be the legislator representing that, not any big deal.

GT 1:01:44 Are you talking about state or national?

Rod 1:01:46 State. It'll take a couple of state legislature seats and it would mean one congressional seat. Now the Democrats have a congressional seat, and they've held it, they've had one. Jim Matheson held that seat for a long time. That was a Republican mistake. When they gerrymandered last, there was Rob Bishop who said, "I don't want all those Democrats in my first district." There was Jason Chaffetz, "I don't want them all." So they ended up putting most of them in the fourth district where there wasn't a Republican to say, "I don't want them." So that was a less Republican district than the other districts and consequently, they've lost it.

GT 1:02:31 Yeah, because originally in 2010, there were only three districts and so then they created the fourth district.

Rod 1:02:35 That's right.

GT 1:02:36 And that's where they put most I guess....

Rod 1:02:38 Well, they put a lot of democrats from West Valley. It isn't a democratic district, but it's a just barely Republican district. So, Jim Matheson could hang on to it, and Ben McAdams could win it. We'll have to wait and see.

GT 1:02:59 Mia Love had that seat.

Rod 1:03:00 Yes, she had that seat twice, two terms, four years, I think. She beat Doug Owens. She beat him twice.

GT 1:03:25 Okay.

Rod 1:03:26 So she had it four years and now McAdams has it and I don't know. They'll make hard run at him this next time.

GT 1:03:38 Because I know that the citizens passed a law that said we want an independent commission.

Rod 1:03:42 That's right.

GT 1:03:43 It seems like the legislature overrode them again.

Rod 1:03:44 No. The legislature hasn't overridden them yet. It doesn't matter. It was passed in 2018, and it doesn't matter until '20. So next winter, they may override them. It is only advisory. The Utah Constitution says, "The legislature shall redistrict." So, everyone agrees that you have a committee, and the committee says, "Well, we think you should cut the districts this way." The legislature could say "Well, thank you for your input," and then do what it wants. So, they could just override them in practice. Or they could change things in advance, either abolish them or do whatever they want. They may do that next winter, or they may just wait and see. I don't know what they'll do. But they very much don't want to give the Democratic Congressional seat. They'd rather not give them an extra couple of legislative seats, too. But that wouldn't make any difference. The Republicans would still have elephantine majorities.

How Utah Politics are Different than the Nation

Introduction

Utah politics are different than national politics in a few different ways. For example, Utah governors enjoy the highest ratings of governors in any state, and state politicians are more concerned with balance budgets than cutting taxes. Does LDS Church culture play a role in this? Rod Decker tells more about how Utah politics are different from the nation. Check out our conversation....

Interview

GT 1:05:02 Alright. Well, the last topic that I thought we could discuss, which I thought was very interesting is in your book, you'd mentioned that Utah governors enjoy a higher approval rating than in pretty much every other state. Why do you think that is?

Rod 1:05:23 The best explanation I've heard was from Mike Leavitt. I asked him about it. He said, "If you do an okay job, they sort of sustain you." Sustain is a Latter-day Saint word. The Latter-day Saints sustain people in their congregations and they always do it unanimously. There is a Latter-day Saint tradition of supporting leaders, and it extends to governors, if you do an okay job. So, Utah has popular governors, more popular than maybe any other state. They're certainly contenders and Utah has long serving governors. The last governor to be defeated--well excuse me. The lieutenant governor I can't--her name will come to me in a minute.

GT 1:06:26 Olene Walker.

Rod 1:06:27 Olene Walker got beat but she wasn't elected. She got beat in convention, she didn't make it to the primary. She wasn't elected. She served the end of Mike Leavitt's term. But the last elected governor defeated was J. Bracken Lee when he ran for a third term. He was beaten in a Republican primary, and then he ran as an independent in the general and got beaten again. That was in 1956, and before that, Herbert Maw when he went for a third term. The last governor not to win a second term was, I think, Rendell Mabey back in the 20s. So Utahns re-elect their governors, and Utah has the longest serving governors, except for Alaska or Hawaii. They didn't start having governors until a lot later. So, we have popular, long-serving governors. Part of the reason is we've been lucky. We've had good governors. Part of the reason is that we have a tradition of supporting leaders.

GT 1:07:48 Okay. I know you also mentioned something about two types of Republicans: tax-cutters and budget balancers.

Rod 1:07:56 Yeah.

GT 1:07:58 Can you tell how that goes in Utah politics?

Rod 1:08:01 Republicans covet tax-cutters and budget-balancers. Utah Republicans are tax-cutters in Washington and budget-balancers in Utah. The Utah legislature and Utah governors are scrupulous about balancing the budget. They're careful. Occasionally, there might be a very small deficit that slips in and they immediately pay it off the next year. They're careful, and they've been that way for decades. They weren't always that way. But they've been that way for decades. But in Washington, all the Utah Republicans voted for Ronald Reagan's tax cuts, voted for Donald Trump's tax cuts, voted for George W. Bush's tax cuts. Now, they say we should cut spending to balance the budget, but they know that's not going to happen. They voted for tax cuts, even though it increased the deficit.

Rod 1:08:57 Now here, they like tax cuts too. They cut taxes, but they don't cut taxes, if it'll make a deficit ever. And they'll raise taxes if they need to balance the budget. In Utah, a balanced budget comes first. In Washington, tax cuts come first. The difference is that Utah Republicans own Utah State Government. They want it to be strong and properly run. Whatever strength Washington has, it's eventually going to be used against us. Put them in deficit. Cut the taxes. Starve the beast. Do everything you can to beat up on them, because even so, even after you've done everything you can, they're going to come out here and run you off federal land or declare a monument or make you allow abortions. I mean, they're going to do bad stuff to you out here. So, you don't want them any stronger than you have to have them.

GT 1:09:59 Yeah. Since you mentioned that, can we talk a little bit about the monument with President Clinton and President Obama and President Trump? Tell us about why Utahns haven't appreciated those presidents.

Rod 1:10:25 Well, Clinton, when he was running for re-election, his pollster came up with the fundamental idea: You need a big environmental surprise, getting toward the election. He had offended some Western environmentalists. It made him worry in Oregon and California. So we'll do a big environmental surprise. They thought what it might be, and they said a big monument in southern Utah. Kathleen McGinty, who was the head of the Council on Environmental Quality for him, his chief economic and environmental advisor, wrote him a confidential memo that said the political purpose behind the monument. She said, "You'll make people in Utah mad. They aren't going to vote for you anyway. Don't worry about them. You'll score points with environmentalists in other western states." It worked out perfectly. He made the monument. He stood in Arizona and made the monument in Utah. He didn't dare come to Utah. Utahns were mad. The only bad thing from a Democratic standpoint was they throw out Bill Orton, who was the only Democratic congressman. But he carried more western states that any Democrat since Lyndon Baines Johnson.

GT 1:12:04 Clinton did.

Rod 1:12:04 Yeah, in his reelection bid. So, it worked out exactly the way it was supposed to. So, there was a big monument down there. Then President Obama, as he left office, created another big monument, the Bears Ears, and they created big monuments in Utah because--the reasoning is similar. The environmental movement is national. We can win. Democrats are environmentalists. We can score with the environmentalists. We pay no political price. Utahns don't vote for us anyway. What the heck? So, we got those two monuments, then President Trump comes in and reduces them, and now it's in federal court and we'll see what happens.

GT 1:12:41 Well, great. Is there anything else we've missed that you'd like to talk about with regards to your book?

Rod 1:13:12 I don't think so. We've talked about a lot. I'll say this. Utah spends the least amount of money on its schools per school child of any state. I tell stories about it in here. Educators and Democrats say Utah should spend more and in fact, Utah gets a little better than average results nationally, but Utah has kids that it ought to get. It's got not so many minority kids. It's got kids with educated parents. It's got kids that live with two parents. All of those things are supposed to raise kids scores and do generally. Other states that are like Utah, do much better than Utah. Utah spends the least and sort of muddles along with a gentleman C.

Rod 1:14:16 It's been 40 years. The modern fight started in the Reagan administration. They did a report called A Nation at Risk,[8] saying that the nation's schools weren't good enough. Almost every state took action in response--Utah a little bit. The Secretary of Education at the time was Terrell Bell from Utah. The chair of the Commission, that did *A Nation at Risk* was David P. Gardner from Utah. So, it was a Utah event, but Utah didn't do much about it. Legislators don't believe in spending money on education. They tell you, "Yes, we spend all we can afford," but in fact, they've cut taxes, cut taxes for schools, cut spending for schools, taken money from schools and put it into roads. They do it and they do it kind of surreptitiously. When no one's looking, they create a new road fund and divert a little money into it. No one pays much attention. Since the 1980s, a long time, 40 years, maybe, Utah has had the lowest spending per school child, and Utah has not very good results. Now legislators say we

---

can improve schools. We could do it without more money. They've got reforms. They've got all these ideas for improving schools, and they do one after another. The educators all say "Yeah, yeah, yeah." Then they never do it. It's just one after another. The legislators are more powerful, but the educators are smarter. But in the end, it doesn't work. Utah kids don't get the education. If they got a better education, their life chances would be better.

GT 1:16:25 Yeah. So is this something do you think? I would think that this would be a family issue. Do you think the LDS Church could tip the scales towards education?

Rod 1:16:37 I'm sure the LDS Church could do stuff. I'm sure they won't. I mean, this isn't the sort of thing they get mixed up in. Most of the people watching, okay, the rule of Utah politics is this. The LDS Church shouldn't mess in politics, except when they're on my side. That's the general rule. Yes, they can get what they want, so you wish they were on your side. Isn't that a family issue? Isn't Medicaid a family issue? Isn't education a family issue? Well, it isn't the sort of thing they get mixed up in. Probably we're better off. Even if we could do better, we're probably better off doing worse than having those guys decide things for us. That's my view.

GT 1:17:30 I swear there was a state legislator and I'm trying to remember his name. Within the last year two and he talked about the LDS Church. He felt like the LDS Church tipped the scales too much in Utah politics.

Rod 1:17:45 There have been a number of legislators. There was a guy named Wimmer. He was a conservative Republican and he used to be a Latter-day Saint. He's become an evangelical, nice guy. He was a conservative legislator up there, and he said that the LDS Church, would--I don't think he used the word bully, but he has said essentially in pretty strong terms. He said that they push people around too much. Steve Urquhart, who was a senator from St. George said the LDS Church threw its weight around too much up there. He had in mind particularly the compromise that the LDS Church worked out with the gay community on the civil rights bill. So there are always some who say the LDS Church has too much power. From the first legislature in 1896, I have legislators saying the LDS Church is too powerful up here.

GT 1:18:53 Unless they're on my side, right?

Rod 1:18:54 Yeah. Unless they're on my side, yeah.

GT 1:19:00 Well, Rod Decker. I really appreciate you talking about your book. Can you give us your famous sign off?

Rod 1:19:08 You're *Gospel Tangents*? Okay. Okay. Rod Decker, *Gospel Tangents*.

GT 1:19:15 Thanks a lot Rod. I appreciate it. I hope you enjoyed our conversation with Rod Decker. Rod, it was a lot of fun, and I hope people buy your book, especially if you're interested in the political history of Utah. It was fun to go clear back to Territorial Legislature all the way through the present day. Check out his book, Utah Politics.[9] It's a lot of fun.

---

[9] Can be purchased at https://amzn.to/34l2puB

Additional Resources:

Check out our other interviews with Paul Reeve & Elder Snow

Elder Steven Snow, Church Historian

Elder Steven Snow served as Church Historian since 2012 & in the First Quorum of Seventy from 2001-2019.

305: Does the Church Hide Historical Documents?
https://gospeltangents.com/2019/08/does-church-hide-documents/

304: Snow on Journals, Issues of Church & State
https://gospeltangents.com/2019/08/snow-journals-church-state/

303: Elder Snow & Gospel Topics Essays
https://gospeltangents.com/2019/07/elder-snows-role-gospel-topics/

302: "I Just Love Church History!"
https://gospeltangents.com/2019/07/i-love-church-history/

Greg Prince on Gays & the Mormon Church

Dr. Greg Prince details the history of LDS political fights over gay marriage from the 1990s through today.

286: Legal & Science Issues on LGBT
https://gospeltangents.com/2019/06/legal-science-social-lgbt/

285: Revelatory Whiplash
https://gospeltangents.com/2019/06/revelatory-whiplash/

284: The Christian Right & LGBT Fight
https://gospeltangents.com/2019/06/christian-right-lgbt-fight/

283: Mixing Church & Politics in Gay Fight
https://gospeltangents.com/2019/06/mixing-church-politics-lgbt-fight/

Dr. Paul Reeve on Black Mormon History in Utah

Dr. Paul Reeve – Prof of History, University of Utah.

009: Dr. Paul Reeve's Role in Race Essay
https://gospeltangents.com/2017/02/27/paul-reeve-wrote-the-race-essay/

008: Dating the LDS Temple and Priesthood Ban
https://gospeltangents.com/2017/02/26/dating-the-lds-priesthood-and-temple-ban/

007: Becoming a Fanboy of Orson Pratt
https://gospeltangents.com/2017/02/24/becoming-a-fanboy-of-orson-pratt/

006: The Black Mormon Scandals
https://gospeltangents.com/2017/02/22/the-black-mormon-scandals/

005: How did Joseph Smith Deal with Muslims?
https://gospeltangents.com/2017/02/19/how-did-joseph-smith-deal-with-muslims/

004: How did Others Deal with Slavery?
https://gospeltangents.com/2017/02/12/how-did-others-deal-with-slavery-blackhistorymonth/

003: How Mormons Became a Racial Category
https://gospeltangents.com/2017/02/09/how-mormons-became-a-racial-category/

Epilogue

You can get our transcripts at our amazon.com author page. I've got a link here, but just do a search for Gospel Tangents interview, and you should be able to find a bunch of them there. Please subscribe at Patreon.com/gospeltangents. For $5 a month, you can hear the entire interview uncut and for $10 you can get a pdf copy. We've also got a $15 tier where if you want a physical copy, I'll be the first to send it to you, so please subscribe at Patreon or on our website at Gospeltangents.com. For our latest updates, please like our page at facebook.com/Gospeltangents and also check our twitter updates Gospel tangents. Please subscribe on our apple podcast page tinyurl.com/GospelTangents, or you can subscribe on your android device. Just do a search for Gospel Tangents. Thanks again for listening. Click here to subscribe, here for transcript and over here we've got some more of our great videos. Thanks again.